GOD'S GRACE

FROM GROUND ZERO

ALSO FROM JIM CYMBALA

Fresh Wind, Fresh Fire
Fresh Faith
Fresh Power
The Life God Blesses

JIM CYMBALA

PASTOR OF THE BROOKLYN TABERNACLE

with Stephen Sorenson

GOD'S GRACE

FROM GROUND ZERO

**SEEKING GOD'S HEART
FOR THE FUTURE OF OUR WORLD**

ZONDERVAN™

GRAND RAPIDS, MICHIGAN 49530

ZONDERVAN™

God's Grace from Ground Zero
Copyright © 2001 by Jim Cymbala

Requests for information should be addressed to:
Zondervan, *Grand Rapids, Michigan 49530*

ISBN: 0–310–23662–2

Published in association with the literary agency of Ann Spangler & Associates, 1420 Pontiac Road SE, Grand Rapids, MI 49506

Interior design by Beth Shagene

Printed in the United States of America

01 02 03 04 05 06 07 08 /❖ DC/ 10 9 8 7 6 5 4 3 2 1

Dedicated to the memory of the firefighters,
police officers, and emergency services personnel who
gave their lives for others on September 11, 2001

CONTENTS

ONE   A Season of Harvest   9

TWO   Truth and Love   25

THREE   Clinging Christians   41

FOUR   Only Today   51

FIVE   Making It Through the Storm   63

SIX   A Strange Blessing   75

ONE

❧

A Season of Harvest

It was almost midnight on Monday, September 10, 2001, when Carol and I finally got into bed for a much-needed night's rest. It had been a busy day following an even busier Sunday at the Brooklyn Tabernacle in New York City, and we were both exhausted. Carol soon dropped off to sleep, but for some reason I lay awake as the hours slowly dragged on. About 2:30 A.M., I got up and went to the study that adjoins our bedroom to read the Bible and pray. I returned to bed sometime after 3:30 A.M., but sleep continued to elude me.

This was very unusual because I have been blessed with the ability to sleep no matter what pressures or challenges might be facing me. But the predawn hours of this Tuesday morning were unlike any before. I watched the clock register 5:00 A.M. Again I arose to pray. Again I returned to bed. Twice I asked the Lord what was happening. I was perplexed. I had taken in no caffeine, no physical problem was present, yet I could not sleep. *Is the Lord wanting to speak to me about something?* I wondered. *Is he preparing me spiritually for some future situation?*

As I lay awake and opened my heart to God, one verse kept burning in my heart all through that long night. It seemed to be an odd message, but I meditated long and hard on its meaning: "He who gathers crops in summer is a wise son, but he who sleeps during harvest is a disgraceful son" (Proverbs 10:5).

The picture here is one that would be especially meaningful to an agricultural nation. Summer is the strategic time for reaping so that all the previous work of tilling the soil and planting the seeds will not be wasted. After all, no one can harvest corn during the cold months of the year. That must be done during *harvest time*. All the sunshine and rain with which God blesses the fields will mean nothing if people don't go out and work hard in the fields during the critical hours. Scripture says that the wise son understands the harvest season and makes the most of it. He cooperates fully with his father's enterprise and goals.

Usually the proverbs make a contrast between those who are *wise* and those who are *foolish*, but in Proverbs 10:5 the language is much stronger. The son who sleeps during harvest season is described as a *disgrace!* The picture here is that of a son who lies around lazily as the critical window of opportunity passes by. All the hard work of sowing seed and the blessings of sun and rain are wasted as valuable crops begin to rot in the fields. The disgraceful son lies sleeping (something I couldn't do that night!) when everything around him cries out for diligent, hard work.

I lay awake applying that verse over and over again to me and to the church I pastor. *Are we sleeping like that dis-*

graceful son? Am I wasting God's window of opportunity and failing the Lord as a shepherd of his sheep? I asked God to forgive me for any lack of fervency on my part. I told him that I didn't want to be a disgraceful son, nor did I want the Brooklyn Tabernacle to fail him during a crucial hour.

The digital clock next to my bed registered 6:20 A.M. before I finally fell off to sleep. The last words echoing in my mind were *It's harvest time.* The new, heightened awareness in my soul from my long night's vigil was *It's harvest time. We must find ways to reach the people in New York City with the gospel of Jesus Christ. Children, teens, adults, senior citizens—they all need God. We must not trifle with secondary matters or live self-indulgently when the fields are so ripe for spiritual reaping.*

CALAMITOUS EVENTS

I had slept only a few hours when I awoke and began to follow the calamitous events unfolding at the World Trade Center on television. Many people from our congregation are employed in this area, and I knew that some of them worked inside the Twin Towers. My wife and I were thinking of them when first one tower, and then the second, came crashing down in a scene that no New Yorker—or any other American—will ever forget.

The phone began ringing off the hook in my home as reports came into the church and were forwarded to me. Within minutes a few members called to say they were okay and had narrowly escaped this national disaster. Still others hadn't been heard from yet. Within an hour or so, some members arrived at the church, covered with soot and dust, shaken and distraught from their close call. Stunned people who had been in or near the financial district made their way across the Brooklyn Bridge into downtown Brooklyn and walked up Flatbush Avenue right past our church. Some were unashamedly crying. Others, fighting to hold in their emotions, stared only straight ahead. They shuffled by quietly, many still covered by debris, their shoes whitened by dust.

The harvest field was ripe with people who suddenly knew at a deep level that they needed God in their lives.

❧

We transferred some of our office staff to the front of our building, where we offered water and other aid. We also opened the church doors so that anyone who wished to could come in and find a place of sanctuary and prayer. A tourist from the Midwest stumbled in, seemingly in a state of shock. We comforted her, helped her plan her next course of action, and reminded her that God hears her prayers.

As the hours passed, I tried to gather my thoughts and emotions. Once again that phrase echoed in the deepest part of my being: *It's harvest time*. The harvest field was ripe with people who suddenly knew at a deep level that they needed God in their lives.

The next few days were tense. Soon we learned that four members of our church were among the missing. But there were other members who miraculously escaped the carnage. A few had experienced unusual delays that kept them from their usual place of work in the World Trade Center that morning. We found ourselves inundated by a seeming tidal wave of pain, sorrow, and fear along with a myriad of unanswered questions. We responded as best we could to help meet the different levels and kinds of need around us. Family members in our church had loved ones still on the list of missing persons. The younger children in our church needed specially designed classes to help them deal with the violence of September 11. Every time I spoke to someone, I realized how much I needed discernment and wisdom in order to understand how the tragedy had impacted that person.

A DEEP WOUNDING AND SPIRITUAL TENDERNESS

I was born and raised in New York City and have pastored in the inner city for nearly thirty years. As well as I know New Yorkers, I could not have imagined the impact these events would have. I knew nothing like this had ever happened before, but I was still amazed by the incredible effects on people during the days following the terrorist attacks. People in a supermarket near my home moved about the aisles in a kind of daze. No one spoke at the checkout counters. Strangers looked at each other with new awareness and feeling in the parking lots, restaurants, and streets of my neighborhood. Even traffic seemed a little slower, drivers a little more careful.

The tragedies had pierced the soul of my city. A deep wounding of its collective heart had transformed a place so famous for its brashness and hard exterior. People everywhere had a new softness, an acute awareness of their mortality and the existence of evil and death.

About a week after the September 11 attacks, this new feeling in the city came home to me in a park about a mile from my home. I had taken a break from my hectic schedule so I could get some physical exercise. Ricky Manga, a friend and staff member of the Brooklyn Tabernacle, and I went to play some paddleball (an outdoor game similar to racquetball). As I approached the park, I noticed a lone policeman sitting in a police car about twenty feet away. I had never seen a policeman stationed there before, so I wondered what was going on. Because of the ongoing terrorism threat, I looked around to try to figure out why he was positioned in that spot, but I couldn't figure it out.

While Ricky and I played, I occasionally glanced at the police car. An hour or so later, the policeman was still there. As we were leaving the park, Ricky and I walked toward the squad car. When the policeman saw us coming, he rolled down the window and said, "Hey, how are you doing?"

"I'm fine," I answered. Then, with heartfelt admiration, I said, "Listen, I can't thank all of you guys for what you did at the World Trade Center, but I can thank you." I stuck out my hand toward him. He reached out through the window with his right hand and shook mine. Ricky also shook his hand.

That moment all three of us were just a half-second away from breaking down in tears. I sure felt it, Ricky felt it, and I saw the policeman blink, too. We all had been affected by an unprecedented sense of sadness that made our hearts acutely sensitive. Talk of God and the benefits of prayer—topics that had been politically incorrect just days earlier—were now on everyone's lips. In every one of Mayor Rudy Giuliani's press conferences, the topic of prayer was mentioned numerous times. Men and women secretly pondered the fact that they could be enjoying coffee and a bagel on the eighty-fifth floor of an office building one morning and have only seconds to live.

It was—and still is—*harvest time* all right, but to a degree that no one could have ever predicted or imagined. Thoughts of millions of people worldwide turned toward the invisible and eternal, to the existence of God and the deep mysteries of life. Issues that a glut of materialism and the frenetic pace of city life had always pushed to the back of people's minds were suddenly front and center. Those who had protested the mention of God and decried the practice of prayer must have been hiding under a rock somewhere because they were not found in public. People everywhere were conscious of their vulnerability and need. Friends reported that this was happening in other parts of the country, too.

But even with these visible changes, I wasn't ready for what occurred during the first Sunday after that infamous day. We had four services as usual in the Brooklyn Tabernacle, and each of them overflowed with people. They sat or stood in every part of our sanctuary and overflow areas. It was wall-to-wall humanity, yet ushers told me that lines of people who could not get in extended down the block outside our church. I exited the sanctuary after one service to find people with heads bowed in prayer standing outside our main lobby. They hadn't even attended church yet that day!

The atmosphere during those Sunday services was incredibly tender and sensitive. We were still missing four members, and hope for their survival was growing dimmer by the day. The congregation and numerous visitors prayed for the families involved as we ministered love and comfort to those directly affected by the attacks. But it was not until I shared the gospel of Jesus Christ that I realized how dramatically the Lord had opened hearts. More than six hundred people that Sunday answered the invitation to yield their lives in simple faith to the Lord. The after-meeting times of confession and surrender were filled with tears and heartfelt praying. It was a great day of spiritual *harvest*. And the harvest continues.

TRUTH SPOKEN IN LOVE

Marjorie, who sings alto in the Brooklyn Tabernacle Choir, had made her faith in Christ evident to her co-workers, but a new opportunity arose on Friday, just three days after the attacks. Marjorie works on Long Island, which is a good distance from where the Twin Towers stood. Although her company was not in harm's way, its employees were still in mourning through the week.

When President Bush declared Friday, September 14, 2001, a national day of prayer, Marjorie asked her manager if all the employees could be called together so she could help lead them in prayer. She also requested and received permission to speak about Jesus Christ. As a result of her love and boldness, God's love invaded her place of employment in a most striking way.

Marjorie ended up sharing with more than one hundred employees the truth of God's great love for them and the need for their names to be written in the Lamb's book of life (Revelation 21:27). Tender hearts responded as she presented the love and truth of Jesus, and *all of them* unashamedly repeated a prayer to accept God's grace in their lives! Their time of prayer together sounded like a beautiful church service, Marjorie said, yet the location was in an office building just outside New York City. This is what can happen when God's truth is spoken in love to hearts the Lord has prepared. If God can use a member of our church like Marjorie in such a remarkable way in an office, what are the opportunities that may be presented to us in the coming days?

AVOIDING DISTRACTIONS

Now is the time for spiritual harvest, and therefore we need to guard against becoming preoccupied with peripheral issues and missing the opportunities to share Jesus' love and compassion with people. During the aftermath of September 11, I was interviewed by many Christian radio stations. One interviewer asked me what seemed to be the most popular question in many Christian circles: "Pastor Cymbala, we've read your books and know of your work there in New York City. Tell us, what is your reading of the disaster at the World Trade Center? Some are saying the *devil did it*, others that *God permitted it*, while still others declare that *God is behind* the whole thing."

I should have known such a question was coming. Make-believe prophets come out of the woodwork during times like these to offer bold proclamations and supposed insights into the latest earth-shattering events. (Remember, for example, when we were *assured* that the USSR was "the bear of the north" mentioned in biblical prophecy, and that it would march down and destroy Israel any day? Now the USSR is no more. In its place poor, beleaguered Russia faces one financial crisis after another!)

> **We need to guard against becoming preoccupied with peripheral issues and missing the opportunities to share Jesus' love and compassion with people.**
>
> ∽

I'm afraid that far too many of us have forgotten what Christianity is really about according to the teaching of the New Testament. Our job is not to be analyzing prophetic charts or splitting theological hairs. Jesus made this abundantly clear during his ministry here on earth. Consider his reaction to some tragic events that occurred during his ministry:

"Now there were some present at that time who told Jesus about the Galileans whose blood Pilate had mixed with their sacrifices" (Luke 13:1). An ugly turn of political events had cost Jewish lives, and the execution of those Galileans was the latest tragedy in Israel. Listen to Jesus' response:

> "Do you think that these Galileans were worse sinners than all the other Galileans because they suffered this way? I tell you, no! But unless you repent, you too will all perish. Or those eighteen who died when the tower in

Siloam fell on them—do you think they were more guilty than all the others living in Jerusalem? I tell you, no! But unless you repent, you too will all perish" (Luke 13:2–5).

The Galileans had probably been killed while offering sacrifices in the temple in Jerusalem. A tower in Siloam toppled, and eighteen innocent lives were tragically lost. Jesus' response to both of these events is a model of how we are to respond to the recent tragedies in our country. The Son of God did not declare who was to *blame* for those events, but used them to warn people lovingly that *they* needed to repent, turn to God, and be saved. He did not explain the *why* of it, but rather used the occasion to again proclaim his never-changing message: "The time has come. . . . The kingdom of God is near. *Repent and believe the good news!*" (Mark 1:15).

As Christians we are followers of Jesus, so we must remember his warning about becoming distracted by secondary matters: "When they [the disciples] met together, they asked him, 'Lord, are you at *this time* going to restore the kingdom to Israel?' He said to them: *'It is not for you to know the times or dates* the Father has set by his own authority. But you will receive power when the Holy Spirit comes on you; *and you will be my witnesses* in Jerusalem, and in all Judea and Samaria, and to the ends of the earth'" (Acts 1:6–8).

Believers in Christ are not supposed to be sitting around smugly discussing *who* is to blame for a national tragedy, nor should we be taken up with the various prophetic interpretations swirling around us. We are far better off to simply obey what Christ commanded us to do: Love hurting, bewildered people and share the good news of eternal life through faith in Jesus Christ. Jesus clearly said that we will never fully understand prophetic times and seasons, nor are those things to be our main concern while living here on planet earth. Our mission as Christians is always the same: To be powerful, compassionate witnesses for Jesus and the gospel of salvation through his name. And I believe we are to do that now as never before.

A KEY REMINDER

There is another truth that is also applicable to the national and international crisis we are facing. Jesus warned, "You *will hear of wars* and *rumors of wars,* but see to it that you are not alarmed. *Such things must happen,* but the end is still to come" (Matthew 24:6). History has proven this prophecy to be exactly true. For more than twenty centuries there has been an endless cycle of wars and rumors of war: tribal wars, ethnic wars, civil wars, and even world wars that enveloped the globe. Jesus didn't say this awful fact of life on earth could be avoided if we Christians prayed in faith or lived godly lives. No, he declared that such things "*must* happen, but the end is still to come."

Just as the United States was attacked at Pearl Harbor and drawn into World War II in 1941, we are now engaged in conflict sixty years later. This new kind of war, a twenty-first-century war, is unlike anything we have ever faced. It began on September 11, 2001, and will probably go on for a long time. The enemy has a diabolical spirit that combines a kamikaze-like madness with genocidal aims worse than Adolph Hitler and the Nazis.

But we must not lose sight of what is most important in these events. God is using them all to remind people in America and in other countries around the world of long-forgotten spiritual truths. Yes, we can say these tragic events in New York City, Washington, D.C., and rural Pennsylvania were a *wake-up call* for our country. That is also true for people in England, France, Germany, Russia, and other countries that might be the next victims of a wave of terrorism.

There is, however, something far more important for us to remember. Jesus didn't leave heaven to condemn and judge the world; he came that the world through him might be saved (John 3:17). He is not trying to destroy people but to save them! Ironically, what the terrorists' blind hatred and kamikaze-like violence meant for evil, God can work for good in order to bring about a vast spiritual harvest of souls. In fact, he already did—at the Brooklyn Tabernacle, where six hundred people put their faith in Christ in one day!

> **It is not the season for fear or flight to some remote hiding place. Rather, it is the season to stand strong and declare our faith in Almighty God.**
>
> ∞

So this is not a time for condemnation and blame. Rather, it is a time for compassion and fresh, bold witnessing for Jesus Christ. It is not the season for fear or flight to some remote hiding place. Rather, it is the season to stand strong and declare our faith in Almighty God.

NEEDED: A NEW KIND OF FERVENCY

There is no doubt that it's harvest time. But let's be honest. We Christians need to see a dramatic change in our level of consecration if we are to reap the harvest spread before us. A new kind of fervency must grip our hearts if we are to make the most of this moment in time. Souls hang in the balance.

Think about what happened on September 11, 2001. More than a dozen men, some of them married, were so filled with hate and violence that they trained for years and gave up their lives to kill thousands of people and live out their fanatical beliefs. In contrast, as the Twin Towers filled with smoke and fire, brave police officers and firefighters by the hundreds entered those buildings to save lives. They knew that only bad things could happen to those structures as the fire and resulting heat rose to incredible levels. But they kept going up *toward* the danger because they were dedicated to rescuing people *from* the danger. It was part of their job.

All of New York City and the entire United States gained a new admiration for these police officers and firefighters. These men and women didn't think of themselves first but performed their jobs while risking their lives. The truth is, the dramatic efforts and dedication they displayed are not as far removed from our lives as we might think. In fact, on a spiritual level, Christians are supposed to be filled with a similar kind of consecration to the task God has put before us.

When the apostle Paul said farewell to leaders from the church in Ephesus, he spoke about his personal devotion to doing God's will and spreading the gospel. He didn't know exactly what the future held, only that "in every city the Holy Spirit warns me that prison and hardships are facing me" (Acts 20:23). We might think that this strange, prophetic confirmation by God's Spirit that only trouble lay ahead would have caused Paul to take a different, safer road to protect himself. Nothing could have been further from the truth. Paul's response calmly revealed his total consecration to Christ: "However, I *consider my life worth nothing to me*, if only I may finish the race and complete the task the Lord Jesus has given me—the task of testifying to the gospel of God's grace" (Acts 20:24).

Consider these powerful words: "I consider my life worth nothing to me"! To our modern ears, they sound strange, even unbelievable. We have been told that serving Jesus Christ will help us live "the good life." We have been led to believe that he would never cause us to leave our comfort zone. But the great apostle reveals to us that this was *never* God's plan for following Christ. In the same way that Jesus fulfilled God's perfect will by giving up his life sacrificially, Paul bravely followed in Christ's footsteps, empowered by the Holy Spirit working in him.

Paul didn't care about comfort zones, nice climates, or even physical well-being. Because he knew he would ultimately live forever with Christ in heaven, his great passion on earth was to "finish the race" and spread the good news of Jesus far and wide. And he would do it regardless of the cost. Like those courageous police officers and firefighters who went *toward* danger to save lives, Paul was not afraid to risk everything to save eternal souls in the name of Jesus.

This same level of dedication is absolutely necessary in the hostile world in which we live today. We Christians and our churches must stop thinking about what's comfortable and begin to take risks in extending ourselves for the Lord. Can we do any less when all around us men and women are displaying such selfless heroism? But we must remember that it will require God's grace and not mere willpower on our part. Only the Holy Spirit can liberate us from the shackles of self-seeking so that we can boldly live our lives for Christ. Let us ask the Lord *today* to change our hearts so that we can work effectively in his fields.

As always, yet as never before, it is harvest time!

TWO

⤝⤞

Truth and Love

ORIGINALLY FROM A SMALL TOWN IN GEORGIA, Dawn Robinson migrated to California after attending Bible school in Tennessee. A gifted singer, she became involved in full-time ministry in California for several years. In 1998 she visited New York City so she could attend the Brooklyn Tabernacle for a few weeks. Her original plan was to resolve some personal problems she was facing, then return to California. But doors seemed to open for Dawn, and she felt God was leading her to remain in New York City. She became a member of the Brooklyn Tabernacle and utilized her musical talent by joining our choir. It didn't take long before Dawn stood out to those in leadership as someone who had a special calling of God upon her life.

How pleased Dawn was when Morgan Stanley, the well-known financial firm, offered her a managerial position. Not only had God given her a great job in a prestigious firm, but she had a stunning view from her office on the sixty-first floor of the World Trade Center in the heart of New York City.

Even though it was not "politically correct" for Dawn to share the gospel in a corporate environment, she began talking about Jesus with a co-worker named Cassie during lunch. For months they discussed Jesus and spiritual things. Dawn clearly laid out the problem of sin in a firm but non-judgmental way. And Cassie freely acknowledged her need for God, but ended every discussion by saying she wasn't quite ready to "get on the bus" and make Jesus her Savior.

WILLING WORKERS ARE NEEDED

We will come back to this story, but first we ought to examine the importance of what Dawn was doing.

Just as Dawn shared her faith with a friend, it is vital that Christians now rise to the spiritual challenge and represent our Lord effectively by boldly speaking his truth in a spirit of love and compassion. Jesus said, "The harvest is plentiful" (Matthew 9:37) about two thousand years ago, when the world's population was quite small. So imagine what he would say now that the world is populated by billions of people, many of whom are newly anxious about an uncertain future.

People today are open, perhaps as never before in history, to discussing issues of life and death, of good and evil, and the meaning of human existence. But are we ready? Let's look at the church's greatest need as we face our new opportunities to share the gospel. Jesus put his finger on it when he declared that "the *workers* are few" (v. 37). Who are these needed workers, and what do they do? They are Christians of all ages who devote themselves whole-heartedly to spreading the gospel and avoid the detours that lead away from the aims of Jesus Christ. They live in the world, they work hard at their jobs, yet their hearts belong not to the world, but to the Lord of the harvest. They share the same passion for lost humanity that Jesus showed when he entered this world and gave his life for our salvation.

It is sad to see how many of us in the church can become confused and miss out on God's grand design for our lives. In the midst of the current crisis of worldwide terrorism, many Christians repeatedly catalog the various sins of our country (and others) as if listing sins is some kind of New Testament ministry. It is not! Christians who do so disobey one of the clearest teachings of Scripture. The apostle Paul shared something very important—something we need to pay close attention to—when he wrote to the Christians in Corinth: "What business is it of mine to *judge those outside the church*? Are you not to judge those inside? *God will judge those outside*" (1 Corinthians 5:12–13).

> **It is sad to see how many of us in the church can become confused and miss out on God's grand design for our lives.**
>
> ❧

We can see what God is saying here if we recall a few basic facts. In the Old Testament the Israelites were God's chosen people, but in the New Testament God's chosen people are all the born-again believers in the universal *Christian church*. Only born-again believers are called "a chosen people, a royal priesthood, a *holy nation*, a people belonging to God" (1 Peter 2:9).

Now, America is neither Israel nor the Christian church. It would be considered biblically to be part of the Gentile nations, although *within* it are true believers who make up part of the body of Christ. Thus it is simply not biblical for Christians to be hurling condemnation at unbelieving sinners, to be judging those *outside* the fellowship of believers. Unfortunately, I have heard that kind of harsh preaching since I was a kid, and it often sounds very righteous and even "prophetic." Some churches and ministries have turned such condemnation into a small industry because many folks like to dwell on "the sins of America." But we Christians have no license to do this from Scripture.

Nowhere in the New Testament do we ever find Paul, Peter, or the other apostles lambasting the nations of the world for their sins. Nor do the apostles blame the nations for disasters or wars that have occurred during every period of history. The New Testament writers certainly dealt honestly with the ugly reality of personal sin, but they always focused on the tenderness of God's grace and pleaded with people to accept Christ's sacrifice for their disobedience.

Unfortunately, when we focus on the sins of people who are *outside* the fellowship of believers, we conveniently divert the searchlight of God's Word and Spirit away from those of us who are *inside* the church. It is we Christians who must be sure our houses are in order because judgment must always "begin with the family of God" (1 Peter 4:17). For example, when was the last time you heard a Christian leader talk about God's warning to those *in* the church who cause division? "Don't you know," Paul wrote, "that you yourselves are God's temple? . . . If anyone destroys [especially by divisiveness] God's temple, *God will destroy him*"

(1 Corinthians 3:16–17). With solemn warnings like these, who has time to lambaste secular humanists who don't even believe in God?

Yes, it is absolutely certain that each human being on earth "is destined to die once, and after that to face judgment" (Hebrews 9:27). But until that great day of judgment, our purpose must be to live Christlike lives in a dark, immoral world and to keep spreading the message of pardon and eternal life through Jesus Christ.

Unconverted sinners in every country and of every race are *supposed* to sin because they *are* sinners by nature. Should we be shocked by all of this? Was the apostle Paul surprised that non-Christians in the Roman Empire lived ungodly lives? Nothing has changed in two thousand years except that there are more unbelievers and sin is even darker.

All of us lived as sinners before Christ changed us. And now Christ has entrusted us—his followers—to share the same message of reconciliation and deliverance we received with other spiritually lost people.

Sharing this message of good news is the main task of Christian ministry and is in keeping with the Spirit of Jesus and the truth of God's Word:

> Since, then, we know what it is to fear the Lord, we try to persuade men.... Therefore, *if anyone is in Christ*, he is a *new creation*; the old has gone, the new has come! All this is from God, who reconciled us to himself through Christ and *gave us the ministry of reconciliation*.... We are therefore Christ's ambassadors, *as though God were making his*

appeal through us. We implore you on Christ's behalf: *Be reconciled to God* (2 Corinthians 5:11, 17–18, 20).

There was a day when God's people were living under the law of Moses and the Old Testament prophets were denouncing the sins of Israel and sometimes even those of surrounding nations. But not today. We are living during the era of God's grace. We are living under the gospel of Jesus Christ, which is powerful enough to change the most hardened, hopeless man or woman.

It is true that America is extremely ungodly in many ways. The same can be said of England, Mexico, Nigeria, and every other nation of the world. But God still loves every person in every land and desperately pursues every person because he has never ceased in his mission to "seek and to save what was lost" (Luke 19:10). As Christians we must do the same.

ONE PERSON AT A TIME

We all hear this talk about our country's need to change. That is true. But how will America (or any other nation) change and become more godly? Before any change can be seen nationally, the men and women who make up that nation must be *transformed individually*. And what else can change people's hearts but the gospel, which is "the power of God for the salvation of *everyone who believes:* first for the Jew, then for the Gentile" (Romans 1:16)? This view might appear to be simplistic to some, but it is the gospel truth! We can denounce sin all we want to, and we can pass all the laws we care to. *Nothing* will fundamentally change in our world until the gospel of Christ triumphs in the hearts and minds of individual people around the globe. This is the essential fact of spiritual life that is clearly outlined in the New Testament.

This truth is also the reason why the Scriptures record in such detail the last moments of Jesus before he ascended back to heaven: "'You will be my witnesses in Jerusalem, and in all Judea and Samaria, and to the ends of the earth.' *After he said this*, he was taken up before their very eyes" (Acts 1:8–9). Jesus knew how wicked people and nations would become in the future. Thus his very last statement reminds us to never lose our focus. In keeping with his final words, we must continue to be witnesses of his love and mercy.

Then why have many in the church lost their way and become hard voices of condemnation instead of Christlike vessels of mercy? The answer is found in another warning Jesus gave to all of us: "Because of the increase of wickedness, *the love of most will grow cold*" (Matthew 24:12). Our Lord spoke of a future day when lawlessness and evil would so proliferate in our world that they would overwhelm our sensitivities and evaporate the love of not just a few people but of *most*! Likewise, the apostle Paul warned of "terrible times in the last days" when people will live "without love" (2 Timothy 3:1, 3). The amazing thing about these words is that these same people who will live without love also will have "a form of godliness" (v. 5)!

I witnessed an example of this one Sunday evening many years ago when a guest preacher was delivering his message at the Brooklyn Tabernacle. As I sat a few feet behind him and listened, a terrible awareness came upon me. He was preaching truth from the Bible, but he was also *very angry.* The decaying morals of our society and the growing luke-warmness in much of the Christian church had pushed him into such an irritated state that it was absolutely impossible for him to speak "the truth *in love*" (Ephesians 4:15).

> **If all of our testimony about Christ is met by rejection, we must still love these same people and always act kindly toward them.**
>
> ❦

This kind of attitude was bad enough then, but it is lethal at this time when harvest and crisis are coming in together.

Right alongside the unfortunate voices focusing only on condemnation and judgment, there were other statements that made me cringe during the aftermath of the terrorist attacks. A well-known, supposedly "Christian" clergyman told a national television audience that it was now time to draw near to God. "So go to your synagogue this weekend," he said, "or go to your mosque, or visit your church and draw near to God." That might be a politically correct statement, but it is nothing that would ever have come out of the mouth of Christ or any of his apostles. The gospel will never fit into a politically correct mold.

We Christians don't have to—and should not—compromise our belief in the New Testament's teaching about our Lord Jesus. We should share with Muslims, Jews, and everyone else the uniqueness of Jesus Christ as Son of God and Savior of the world. We must tell how he died and rose again from the dead according to Scripture. We should also talk about the difference he has made in our lives. Yet, if all of our testimony about Christ is met by rejection, we must still love these same people and always act kindly toward them. Would Jesus have us do anything else?

As someone with great insight once said, "Love without truth is hypocrisy, and truth without love is brutality." We will avoid both extremes by asking God for grace and wisdom so we can speak *the truth* in love.

OPPORTUNITIES

About a week after the World Trade Center horror, a Middle-Eastern, Arabic-speaking family appeared at our church to enroll in our adult literacy program, which is open to the whole community. The women were dressed in traditional Muslim garb with veils and long gowns. The director of our program spoke with them because registration had ended for current classes. Although their reading and writing skills were too advanced for the program, they pleaded to be included. They wanted to take the three-nights-a-week course so they could improve their English writing skills.

As she talked with them further, the program director learned they were also frightened by the verbal threats they had encountered since September 11. The husband told her, "We are not all like that. We are not all terrorists!" Recognizing that God might be working in their lives, she welcomed them into the program. Now, three nights a week this Muslim family is being surrounded by Christians, the Bible, and the gospel of Christ! Isn't this how Jesus would want us to respond? Who knows if world events, combined with love-filled churches and ministries, will produce a harvest of Muslim men and women for our Lord Jesus Christ? Hasn't his heart been longing after them all these years? Oh, may we make the most of this special moment in our nation's history!

AN INSIDE LOOK

And that brings us back to Dawn Robinson, the woman whose passion for the harvest dramatically affected her friendship with a co-worker.

Dawn Robinson began her day on Tuesday, September 11, in the usual way, by taking the express bus from her apartment in Brooklyn to 2 World Trade Center—the South Tower. She then rode the elevator up to the forty-fourth-floor plaza and transferred to another bank of elevators that took her to her office on the sixty-first floor. It was a beautiful, crystal-clear day when she looked out her window at 7:30 A.M. and began working.

After more than an hour, Dawn looked out the window on her right side, which overlooked the East River. "I heard a strange whistling sound that sounded like it was coming directly at me," she says. "I looked up and thought I saw something huge for just a split second. Then I felt a slight jolt. I jumped to my feet and saw that chunks of debris seemed to be falling from the North Tower.

"Some of my co-workers and I stared out the windows trying to figure out what was going on. Suddenly two huge fireballs shot past my window, and everyone began to run toward the nearest elevators. Eight people rode down with me to the forty-fourth floor plaza, which was as low as we could go on that elevator." Oddly, when Dawn reached the forty-fourth floor, there was a party-like atmosphere. Morgan Stanley employees always went to that floor during the many fire drills conducted in the building since the infamous 1993 World Trade Center bombing incident.

"Workers from other floors were conversing and laughing with one another. It seemed like a routine fire drill that had turned into a huge coffee break. We felt no sense of alarm or danger. Whatever we had seen and felt on the sixty-first floor, everything now seemed to be under control."

Dawn joined in the chatter with others. Some people conjectured that the North Tower must have experienced some type of problem, and within minutes an announcement came over the loudspeakers that everything was, in fact, under control.

"We were instructed either to continue to the forty-fourth-floor cafeteria or to return to our workstations. I saw no one leave at this point. There was no need for alarm, because those in authority had confirmed that everything was secure. So I worked my way through the milling crowd of people toward the bank of elevators that would take me back to my office.

"As the elevator doors opened, I stopped suddenly, feeling an urgent sense of alarm and even claustrophobia. *How could this be*, I wondered, *since the all-clear signal has been given? Besides, my wallet, identification card, credit cards, and the keys to my apartment and car are in my office. How can I not go back up to retrieve them?"*

But something was telling Dawn to quickly leave the South Tower, so she turned away from the elevator, made her way through the relaxed crowd, and convinced a few friends to come with her. About 9:00 A.M., they entered the stairwell on the forty-fourth floor to exit 2 World Trade Center.

"Other people were walking slowly down the stairs with us, but no one was panicking. Just as we reached the forty-second floor, a tremendous impact threw us against the wall. Screams of terror filled the air."

United Airlines Flight 175 had just crashed into the South Tower some twenty floors above where Dawn would have been sitting in her office.

"Pandemonium broke out in the stairwell as people pushed to get past one another. I'm only four feet nine inches tall, and the crush of bodies almost toppled me as I grabbed the banister and held on for dear life." Soon the screams were replaced by an eerie silence in the stairwell as the frightened people walked down.

"As I walked, I prayed out loud, 'God, please protect us! Dear Jesus, keep us safe!'"

Her lone, prayerful voice resonated in the quiet, congested stairwell. As she descended, more people joined them. Water and smoke did, too, making the descent more treacherous. It took more than forty-five minutes for Dawn and her friends to reach the smoke-filled concourse level, which had no lights.

"I saw a group of policemen and firemen, but I was mainly thinking about the fastest way to get out of the building. I tried two doors, but couldn't get out because they were blocked by fallen debris. People around me were frantically running in all directions trying to find some way—any way—out of the South Tower. I felt trapped, too, and wondered if I would survive."

Policemen began yelling for people to walk up two non-functioning escalators to the second level. Crowds of workers fought to run up the steps, but progress was difficult and slow. When Dawn and her friends reached the top, they were directed to doors that led outside and were cautioned to stay close to the outer walls of the South Tower to avoid being hit by debris.

"Once we got outside, we did as the policemen told us to do, but we also realized that sooner or later we would have to make a run for it. I darted out away from the building just as some light debris struck me. Then I saw a river of blood on one side of me. On the other, a man with outstretched hands staggered toward me. His face was severely burned. His eyes were sealed shut, and flesh hung loosely from his body. Horrified, knowing I couldn't do anything to help him and certain that medical people would be coming, I kept running as he headed back toward the South Tower."

The formerly blue sky was now gray and turning darker by the second. As Dawn ran down a panic-filled street, explosions went off behind her. "I thought about jumping into the nearby river, but it was pitch black from falling debris. Suddenly I heard the loudest explosion of all."

Within seconds the entire South Tower, unable to hold the 110,000-ton weight of its damaged top section, pancaked floor by floor to the ground.

"As I ran, the huge, dark cloud of debris began chasing me. Hearing jet airplanes, I kept wondering if they were enemy forces bombing us. I didn't know where to hide.

"Suddenly the sky seemed as dark as midnight. The choking cloud overtook me. Everyone around me looked like they'd been draped in white blankets. Dust and soot completely covered us. We were gagging, trying to breathe. Once again I thought I would die. I looked around and could only find one of my co-workers, Cassie. She had grabbed a fireman's arm and had literally been dragged away from the area.

"Cassie and I started running together, as fast as we could, and finally jumped into an abandoned city bus. The huge cloud of dust still filled the air, but the bus windows had kept most of it out."

Huddled with her friend on that bus in downtown Manhattan, Dawn pleaded, "We can't be sure we will survive this. Please, Cassie, don't wait one minute more! Invite Jesus Christ into your life right now!" So, in the midst of the terror and uncertainty, and layered with dust, Cassie prayed out loud and received Christ as her Savior—on a bus.

A few minutes later, Dawn and Cassie made their way toward the Brooklyn Bridge. Dawn was not sure they should cross it, because she thought it might be bombed, too. But they decided to join the mass of people streaming over it into Brooklyn. After being cleaned off at a first-aid station, the two women walked up Flatbush Avenue to the Brooklyn Tabernacle, where our staff workers were literally giving out cups of cold water in Jesus' name.

One of my staff members later told me that, when he handed Dawn some water, she was shaking so badly she could hardly hold the glass. And when he asked her what had happened, Dawn had to wrap her left arm around a light pole to be able to stand up long enough to respond. But she was alive.

Alive—and in the midst of this disaster God used her to share his love with a friend.

Perhaps as you read Dawn's story, your tears flowed. Mine did, and so did the tears of others who helped me with this chapter. But how will we, as Christians, respond any differently from now on? Weeks and months will pass, dimming memories of September 11, 2001. But for Dawn and Cassie and so many others, the memories of what happened that day—and the ways in which their hearts were touched—will never grow dim.

> **In the midst of this disaster God used Dawn to share his love with a friend.**
>
> ❧

I pray that I, as a pastor, will continue to share the simple message of the gospel, which is more powerful than any two-edged sword. I pray that I will remain sensitive to the people who have been directly or indirectly impacted by the events of that tragic day—and by other painful situations. And I pray that you, too, will be open to God's leading as you spend time with co-workers, neighbors, family.... We never know how long we will have on this earth.

No matter what happens, let's ask God to give us many opportunities to invite people to "get on the bus" so they can receive pardon for their sins and look forward to eternity in heaven with Christ.

✌

Dear Father, the fields are ripe for harvest, and we want to be workers you can use. Change the way we think and live. Fill us with your love and power. Take away judgmentalism and fear, and make us bold as we reach out in compassion to people for whom you died. Do this all for Christ's sake. Amen.

THREE

∞

Clinging Christians

Walwyn Stuart started attending the Brooklyn Tabernacle nine years ago. A native of Brooklyn and a member of the New York City Police Department, he was a joyful Christian whose broad smile lit up any room he entered. I remember often greeting him with a Christian embrace and sensing the spiritual and emotional vitality he possessed.

Walwyn met and fell in love with Thelma, a lovely lady from Jamaica, West Indies, who also attended our church. When they married, they proved once again that opposites can attract. Thelma came from a reserved family in which there was not much emotional expression. Members of her family knew they loved each other, but affectionate hugs and kisses were not exchanged every day. Walwyn, on the other hand, loved to hug and kiss his wife no matter where they were or what they were doing.

Walwyn would even cling to Thelma while she washed dishes or was occupied with other duties. She would become so exasperated by his constant show of affection that she sometimes playfully pushed him away and said,

"Leave me alone!" But nothing could stop Walwyn from expressing his love. He would reply, "Don't push me away. You never know how long I'll be around. When I'm gone, I won't be able to hug and kiss you anymore."

When Walwyn and Thelma decided to start a family, he felt it would be wise to make a career change. "Honey," he said, "I'm going to leave the narcotics division and transfer to the Port Authority Police Department. A job with them will be a lot safer than what I'm doing now." So Walwyn became a Port Authority officer in the PATH Division, which often involved assignments in downtown Manhattan.

> **"You know, Pastor—
> I sure wish
> I had one of those
> hugs right now."**
> ✆

When a baby girl was born to Thelma and Walwyn, his affectionate nature seemed to double in strength. Now his embraces smothered not only his wife but also his adorable daughter, Amanda. Soon little Amanda was playfully pushing Daddy away just like her mommy as he swooped in for yet another round of hugs and kisses. And she wasn't even a year old!

By this time Thelma had earned her master's degree in social work and was working just a few blocks away from her husband on the southern tip of Manhattan. They had bought a house on Long Island, which enabled them to have a reasonable commute to the city. Well-organized Walwyn carefully made sure that every bill was paid promptly and kept proper records. He also conscientiously took time each day to read the Bible and spend time with the Lord in prayer.

On Tuesday morning, September 11, 2001, Walwyn responded to the disaster at the Twin Towers. As a member of the Port Authority force, he must have arrived sooner rather than later. He was one of those brave police officers and firefighters who kept going upward into the buildings to make rescues while office workers were heading downward to flee the scene as quickly as possible. Like so many of the rescue workers, he gave his life for the sake of others.

Walwyn never got the chance to see his daughter celebrate her first birthday on September 28, 2001.

Thelma sat in my office ten days after the tragedy. Together we reminisced about Walwyn and his intense love for the Lord and his family. She remembered all those hugs and kisses. She remembered how closely Walwyn would cling to Amanda and her. "You know, Pastor," she said tearfully, "I sure wish I had one of those hugs right now."

CLINGING TO GOD

The manner in which Walwyn expressed his devotion to his family is a great illustration of one of the most powerful phrases in Scripture. These words have to do with the relationship God wants to have with his people: ". . . that you may *love the LORD* your God, that you may *obey His voice*, and that *you may cling* to Him, for *He is your life* and the length of your days" (Deuteronomy 30:20 NKJV).

Moses gave these instructions as he was finishing up his farewell address to the people of Israel. Forty years had passed since God had delivered them from slavery in Egypt. Moses had been recalling the Lord's dealings with them and his great faithfulness. Toward the end of his long message, he pleaded with the Israelites to take it all to heart and serve the God who loved them so much.

To choose to serve the Lord is to choose the blessing of life. To turn one's back on God and worship other gods is to choose death and destruction. So Moses implored the people to choose God, to choose blessing and life by loving the Lord and listening to his voice. But that was not all. Moses said the deepest way they could express their love for God and their obedience to him would be to "*cling* to him."

The word translated "cling" in the New King James Version is translated "hold fast" (NIV, NASB) and "cleave" (KJV). It is the same strong and intimate word used in Genesis 2:24: "For this reason a man will leave his father and mother and *be united* [cling, cleave] to his wife, and they will become one flesh." God obviously desires a deep, spiritual intimacy and oneness of heart with his people.

This kind of intimate, clinging relationship saved certain Israelites when God punished some of his people for their immorality and idolatry. We read in Deuteronomy 4:3–4, "The LORD your God destroyed from among you everyone who followed the Baal of Peor, *but all of you who held fast* [clung, adhered, stayed united] to the LORD your God are still alive today." In other words, salvation and deliverance came to those who continued to cling to the Lord regardless of what other people chose to do.

Now, this can't be brushed off as some obscure and antiquated concept, because it also appears in a New Testament setting. A marvelous Christian church had been founded in

Antioch in Syria during the early days of gospel witness recorded in the book of Acts. The older, established church in Jerusalem had heard great reports of multitudes turning to Christ in Antioch, so they sent a trusted man named Barnabas to visit the young assembly of believers. "When he [Barnabas] arrived and saw the evidence of the grace of God, he was glad and encouraged them all to *remain true* [cleave, cling] to the Lord *with all their hearts*" (Acts 11:23). Their place of safety and strength was to be found in clinging to the Lord every hour of every day.

This idea of our clinging to God in love makes perfect sense when we think about God's awesome love for us. What could please his divine heart more than for each of us to love him back by perpetually clinging to him in trust and devotion? The image that comes to mind is of a mother who is filled with joy as she nurses and cherishes her clinging infant, who in turn finds satisfaction and security in her. Such clinging was the secret underlying the simplicity and power of the early church. It also describes those believers whom the Lord has especially used throughout church history. They were all *clinging* Christians!

As Christians face the twenty-first century, with its unforeseen challenges and opportunities, we must pray for a spiritual revival. The kind of renewal needed is one that will restore an *inward, heart devotion* to Christ that expresses itself in a constant clinging to the Lord. As Deuteronomy 30:20 reminds us, "The LORD is your life"! When we are not clinging closely, but drifting from the Lord, we are moving away from "life" itself.

No wonder the psalmist affirmed, "But as for me, it is good to be *near God*" (Psalm 73:28). He was a servant of the Lord, but he also knew the vital importance of being "near God." I am afraid that many of us today no longer recognize the importance of being "near God." Going to church on Sunday doesn't necessarily mean that we live *near* God. Knowing all kinds of Scriptures and doctrinal positions doesn't make me a *clinging* Christian, either.

The truth is, not all of us continually live near God. Otherwise, why would Scripture invite us to "draw near to God with a sincere heart in full assurance of faith" (Hebrews 10:22)? Or why would we need to be encouraged, as James succinctly entreats us, to "*come near* to God and *he will come near* to you" (James 4:8)?

> **When we are not clinging closely, but drifting from the Lord, we are moving away from "life" itself.**
> ❧

It is quite possible for us to believe in Christ but to live on the fringes of the outer courtyard in a spiritual sense. Yet God invites us to dwell near him in the Holy of Holies. We all know that when a man and a woman are in love, they want to be near one another, not far away. That is exactly how God feels about us, and it is probably the most marvelous fact in the universe. Imperfect as I am, the Almighty delights in me and wants me to constantly cling to him!

Can you imagine how different our lives would be if we just concentrated on holding fast to the Lord and cried out like a baby when anything pulled us away? What peace and joy would be our daily portion! What indelible impressions we would make on people searching for spiritual direction!

Constant clinging to God is the only antidote to the listless, empty living so many of us experience. We have been spiritually born again so we can live near God and cling to him desperately for our daily portion of grace and strength. Understanding doctrinal positions is important. It's even better to know the Bible. But what good are these things if we do not end up drawing near to God? It's one thing to know truth *about* God; it's another thing to live in intimate communion *with* the Lord.

Thousands of people walk through the doors of the Brooklyn Tabernacle each week, but what kind of ministry does it have if it doesn't produce clinging Christians? If our church services have high moments of sincere praise and moving times of spiritual reflection, we should be thankful for these sure signs of God's grace. But we must go much further. We must obey the admonition the prophet Hosea gave more than twenty-five hundred years ago: "So let us *know*, let us press on to *know* the LORD" (Hosea 6:3 NASB). Knowing the Lord . . . clinging to the Lord . . . this is what God really desires for us. This is what delights his heart.

Some people might think that clinging to God means missing out on all the "fun things" life offers. One might imagine that "you can't do this, and you can't go there" because constantly staying close to God will really hamper the "good life" most people are pursuing. Nothing could be further from the truth! When you and I live as clinging Christians, we will experience the fullness of meaning behind the scriptural phrase, "Christ, who is your life" (Colossians 3:4).

We weren't created to get our peace and joy from the cheap toys and shallow pleasures of this world. We were created *for* God. When we abide near him, we will experience firsthand the overflowing inner peace and joy he has always wanted us to possess.

> **Clinging believers know that for every stream of grief that flows into our lives there is a deeper river of peace that comes from the Holy Spirit.**
>
> ∽

The simple rule of life for clinging Christians is that we can go anywhere and do anything ... as long as those things don't offend God's tender, holy heart. Nothing that creates separation between ourselves and the Lord—nothing that spoils our communion and intimacy with him—is allowed. If it drives our precious Lord away, it *cannot* be good for us. Living near God means being sensitive to anything that will "grieve the Holy Spirit of God" (Ephesians 4:30). Only love, not legal commands, will keep us clinging tightly to God.

This kind of intimacy with the Lord brings comfort during the most difficult seasons of life, as Thelma Stuart is now finding out. When we keep clinging to our Lord, we will experience the reality behind the seeming contradiction in the apostle Paul's phrase, "sorrowful, yet always rejoicing" (2 Corinthians 6:10). By living near God we learn that it's entirely possible for us to experience intermittent waves of emotional and mental pain, yet to steadily rejoice in the deepest part of our spirit. Clinging believers know that for every stream of grief that flows into our lives there is a deeper river of peace that comes from the Holy Spirit.

As we hold fast to the Lord in faith and love, he will also give us supernatural direction and guidance. I can honestly tell Thelma that there *are* answers to all the questions that swirl around her during these trying times. What does she do now? How will she raise little Amanda all by herself? God knows that Thelma is facing these and a thousand more perplexities right now. But he *has* answers. He has a plan for her life no matter what Satan might suggest to the contrary. All Thelma has to do is cling closely to Jesus, and the Lord will whisper the right word at the right time.

MOMENTS TO REMEMBER

Less than two weeks after the day Walwyn Stuart lost his life at Ground Zero, I invited Thelma to bring Amanda up to the platform in front of the congregation during our early Sunday morning service. I wanted our church family to know more about Thelma and to explain what she was facing. I also wanted her to see that the body of Christ was standing with her in prayer and practical support.

Thelma and Amanda were not alone on the platform that day. Thelma's father and sister and the pastoral staff stood behind her. But more important to Thelma than the meaningful support of her family and the congregation is the fact that God continues to stand with her as she faces the future. He will, as promised, be her *life*, her *comfort*, and her *strength* no matter what tomorrow might bring. And her little daughter *will* grow up with God's blessing upon her.

On the platform that Sunday morning, I took Amanda from Thelma and held the beautiful girl in my arms as we worshiped God through very real tears and sought his help in the day of trouble. When I spoke a few final words to the congregation, Amanda reached out and tried to grab the microphone I held in my right hand. As I gently pushed her hand away, her reflex was to slide both her tiny little arms around my shoulder and calmly cling to me. There's a lot of her mother in little Amanda, to be sure, but that clinging hug told me there's a strong influence from her dad, too. As she nestled into the protective arms of her pastor, a quiet promise was affirmed in our hearts that God himself would continue to hold her and love her always and provide for that place left empty in her little life.

FOUR

Only Today

Life in our country will never be the same as it was before September 11, 2001. The horrible tragedies at the World Trade Center and the Pentagon had a vast ripple effect that has rearranged much of how we think and live. Prospects for the future seem to indicate that things will continue to change in possibly even more dramatic ways.

The reality of these changes struck home to me in a powerful way when I took an airline flight less than two weeks after the terrorist attacks. The atmosphere at John F. Kennedy Airport bore witness to the new facts of life we face. Hardly anyone spoke as we waited patiently in the rather long line in front of the check-in counter. Most travelers stared aimlessly into space. A few others seemed to be nervously screening every person in line as if they were part of the expanded security team. A newly installed sign informed us about all the items no longer permitted on board an aircraft. I was required to present my photo ID at three different checkpoints before I boarded my flight.

As we taxied away from the gate, the pilot thanked us for flying that day, gave the usual flight information, and added, "We're going to get you to Tampa comfortably and *safely*." A burst of applause broke out in the half-filled cabin. This flight was certainly like none other I had ever been on!

During the two-and-one-half-hour flight I noticed something else rather strange. Conversation was at a bare minimum, and it seemed that passengers were not leaving their seats for *any* reason. I accidentally spilled ink from a highlighter pen on my hand, so I got up to use the washroom. Immediately nervous eyes stared at me as if to say, "Why are *you* walking in the aisle? Get back to your seat!" I could almost hear the collective sigh of relief when I returned a few minutes later. We arrived in Tampa safely and on time, but *routine* would be the last word I would use to describe that flight.

NO GUARANTEES OF A TOMORROW

The terrorist attacks on the United States have altered our lives in much more profound ways than airport procedures for commercial airline flights. God is using the present turmoil to remind us of these words of wisdom given many centuries ago: "Do not boast about *tomorrow*, for you do not know what a day may bring forth" (Proverbs 27:1). What Solomon declared under God's inspiration, people throughout America—and other countries—are taking to heart now as never before in history. Recent events have painfully shattered the smug confidence that *tomorrow* is somehow guaranteed to us.

Did the passengers who boarded the four fateful airline flights on September 11, 2001, ever imagine that it was the last day of their lives? Did the men and women employed at the Pentagon and the thousands of others employed at the World Trade Center that day have any clue that they would never see their families again?

These are not rhetorical questions asked for melodramatic effect in the face of tragedy. Rather, they point us toward an important truth rooted in Holy Scripture.

Not one of us knows what a single day may bring forth. Yet we often live as if seeing tomorrow is a sure thing. We easily forget that "each man's life is but a breath" (Psalm 39:5). Truly we live a brief, fragile existence. Our life is something that "springs up like a flower and withers away; like a fleeting shadow, [it] does not endure" (Job 14:2).

> **Not one of us knows what a single day may bring forth. Yet we often live as if seeing tomorrow is a sure thing.**
>
> ❧

I am not presenting a gloomy philosophy of life. I am expressing the only attitude, as the apostle James wrote, that is proper before God:

> Now listen, you who say, "Today or tomorrow we will go to this or that city, spend a year there, carry on business and make money." Why, *you do not even know what will happen tomorrow*. What is your life? You are a *mist* that appears for a little while and then vanishes. Instead, you ought to say, "If it is the Lord's will, we will live and do this or that!" As it is, you boast and brag. All such boasting is *evil* (James 4:13–16).

"Lord willing" is a phrase I heard often as a child. When other Christians visited my parents' home and spoke about future plans, they would say something like this: "We will attend our niece's wedding in June, Lord willing." I didn't grasp the significance of those two little words until I was much older.

Some people today dismiss the phrase "Lord willing" as trite, religious verbiage, but it is not. It is the truth. The Bible clearly instructs us that it is wise to recognize God's sovereign hand in our plans for tomorrow. The *only* day we really have is today. Yesterday is gone, and we have no guarantee of a tomorrow. So whatever we feel is most important and whatever we purpose to accomplish, we *must* begin to do today!

I've been a pastor for about thirty years and have counseled many folks. Despite the number of people and variety of situations, I encounter a recurring problem as I try to offer biblical solutions to their dilemmas and guide them into God's truth. Men and women from all walks of life are often immobilized spiritually and emotionally by either the past or the future—or both.

Many people, for example, are paralyzed by the past—what happened back then, what someone once did to hurt them, what inequity of life befell them. Of course, the problem with all this is that these things have already happened, and we can't change one detail of it. Every one of us has bad memories and scars, but for God's sake and our own we must learn to get past these hurts by giving them to Christ. Otherwise we will never live for today! Today is the only real day we have, but we can miss out on really living it because of being paralyzed by the past.

Even sadder are those of us who are troubled by anxiety and fear because of what tomorrow might bring—a day we might never see! Jesus told us plainly, "Do not worry about tomorrow, for tomorrow will worry about itself" (Matthew 6:34). We can never fully live in God's only day—*today*—if our nerves are frayed by questions we can't answer: "What will happen to the economy?" "Will there be layoffs that affect me?" "Will terror and death strike again soon?"

God wants us to focus on today. That is why Jesus taught his disciples to pray, "Give us *today* our *daily* bread" (Matthew 6:11). God's way isn't to provide next week's or next year's supply. His way is for us to walk with him daily and trust him for today's necessities. His provision might mean bread, spiritual strength, or peace for a troubled heart. He has everything his people need, and he will provide it for us *day by day*.

The recent, tragic events have made us realize how foolish it is to join with the ungodly who say, "Tomorrow will be like today, or even far better" (Isaiah 56:12). While unbelievers are processing these facts of life, we who are Christians would do well to consecrate ourselves to living wholeheartedly one day at a time.

The only day you can hear God's voice is today. Scripture warns, "*Today*, if you hear his voice, do not harden your hearts" (Hebrews 3:7–8). The only day we can encourage another believer to stay true to Christ is today: "But encourage one another *daily*, as long as it is called *Today*, so that none of you may be hardened by sin's deceitfulness" (Hebrews 3:13). In fact, when the Israelites failed through unbelief to enter God's rest, the Scriptures tell us that God chose another unique day when people who trusted him could experience the fullness of his promise. It wasn't a Saturday, Sunday, or any other day of our week: "Therefore God again set a certain day, calling it Today" (Hebrews 4:7).

Today is the day of salvation. Today is the only day when a person can trust Christ to be his or her Savior and Lord. Today is the only day I can read my Bible and draw nearer to the Lord. Today is the only day I can witness about Christ to a friend or relative. Today is the only day I can pray to God while standing on the promise that "Jesus Christ is the same yesterday and *today* and forever" (Hebrews 13:8).

Yesterday is gone forever, and tomorrow we don't know about, but today is the one day you and I can serve God with everything in us. Today is the only day we can do God's will and live out this verse: "Therefore, do not be foolish but understand what the Lord's will is" (Ephesians 5:17). God's plan for yesterday is history, and who knows if tomorrow will even happen? So we must pursue his will for our lives *today* as he helps us by providing timely grace.

IMPORTANT QUESTIONS, IMPORTANT ACTIONS

Do you love your wife or husband? Then share with him or her how you feel *today*. Is your heart filled with gratitude for a mom or dad who has cared for you faithfully through the years? The only day your parents can hear you express your thankfulness is today. I'm afraid that too many of us are letting our *todays* slip by through mechanical and superficial living that doesn't really come from the heart. The Lord knew this would be a problem for us, so he gave this inspired word: "Whatever you do, work at it with all your heart" (Colossians 3:23). Today is the only day we have to obey that command.

> **Too many of us are letting our *todays* slip by through mechanical and superficial living that doesn't really come from the heart.**
>
> ❧

A striking illustration of this powerful truth impacted my life years ago. While I was attending the University of Rhode Island in 1965, my educational experience required that I watch the movie adaptation of a famous Broadway musical, *Carousel*. As one of several hit musicals written by Richard Rodgers and Oscar Hammerstein, *Carousel* might have been well known to Broadway musical buffs, but I had never heard of it. I was in my early twenties and was the starting point guard for the URI basketball team. Watching people sing to each other and dance around a stage was not my idea of a good time. So I settled in for what I was sure would be a very long couple of hours.

Little did I know the effect the simple story line would have on me.

Carousel is about an uneducated carnival worker named Billy Bigelow who has, in Broadway parlance, a good heart. But he is also part scoundrel. Billy is immature, impetuous, and full of himself. Even though his life is going nowhere and he hangs around undesirable characters, a young, beautiful, and innocent girl named Julie begins to fall in love with him. Her friends try to steer her away from Billy, but as they say, love is blind.

Billy starts to care for Julie, which is difficult for a person as self-centered as he is. One evening they take a moonlit walk, and Julie tries falteringly to tell Billy how she feels. Her honest emotions spill out as she relates how her life has changed since she met him. He takes it all in, but Julie becomes timid and holds back from fully expressing her tender heart.

Billy is strangely moved by her words and tries to open up to her. He wants Julie to know that his life has been different lately, too. But his sense of machismo and his inability to ever seem vulnerable hinders him. He desperately wants Julie to know how he feels, but then again, he doesn't. Caught up in this inner contradiction, Billy sings a beautiful love song to her, but he adapts it to fit his confused state of mind. Yes, he tells her, I, too, *would* feel thrilled just to see you; I *would* get excited at the mention of your name; I *would* dream of spending my life with you. Yet he can't quite express how deeply he feels. So the song becomes "*If* I Loved You." All he can say is, "It would definitely be exciting and wonderful, *if* I loved you."

Billy and Julie eventually marry. Soon afterward she becomes pregnant, but then he is tragically killed in an incident involving some of his unsavory friends. Julie, a pregnant widow, faces the future all alone.

The next scene fast forwards to heaven (!), where Billy went after death. (I told you this is from Broadway, not the Bible.) Seventeen years have passed, and an angel—dressed in civilian clothes—tells Billy, "You know, Billy, everyone up here has a chance to go back for one day, and you might want to consider it. It seems your daughter has taken after you in a lot of ways, and she sure needs some help about now."

Billy doesn't like the implications of these words, but he is able to look down and see that life is pretty difficult for Louise, the daughter he never had a chance to love. Besides being headstrong and rambunctious, she has to endure taunting from her peers who say nasty things about the father she never knew. Louise and her mom also don't have much money or much respect from other folks in town.

Billy realizes that his absence is proving to be very costly, especially for his daughter, who is heading quickly down the wrong road.

"If I go back down, will they be able to see me?" Billy asks.

"Only if you want them to," replies the angel.

So Billy returns to earth for one day to try to make amends for his failures. He approaches his daughter and introduces himself as someone who knew her late father. Louise asks what kind of man her father really was, but Billy has a difficult time finding anything positive to say about his own life!

"You never knew my dad," she blurts out. "The other kids are probably right when they say he died a good-for-nothing!"

This puts Billy over the edge. A heated argument ensues between him and his angry, confused daughter. Billy soon becomes so incensed that he slaps Louise, and she runs back into her house to tell her mother.

"Well, there you go messing up things again!" the angel chides Billy. "Just when she needs you most, you miss the chance to do something kind and helpful."

Suddenly Billy realizes that Julie is coming outside to see the stranger who spoke so rudely and struck her daughter.

"I don't want her to see me!" Billy tells the angel.

"Then she won't," the angel quickly replies.

Julie walks back and forth in front of the house, wondering how this mysterious man disappeared so quickly. "You say he got angry real quick and slapped your face?" Julie asks her daughter.

"Yes, Mom, he did. But the slap didn't hurt like usual. There was something different about it."

> You and I have only one day to do what God is calling us to do, and that day is today.
> ❧

Julie sends her daughter back into the house so she can be alone. Billy is standing only a few feet from Julie, but she can't see him. Yet there's a strange look in her eyes, so you know she's convinced that no ordinary man spoke with her daughter.

Billy draws near and gazes intently at Julie's still-beautiful face. She has done her best to raise their daughter. She has always perfectly defended her late husband's reputation even though at times she knew better. She was left all alone by his sudden death, but she has never complained or faltered. Now Billy stands invisibly next to her as time runs out on his one-day visit to earth.

Billy Bigelow sings one last, beautiful song to his wife before he leaves. It's the same ballad he sang earlier, but now his lyrics are honest. No longer does he sing, "*If* I loved you." He now confesses, "*How* I loved you!" The shame is that Julie can't see or hear Billy (although she somehow senses he is near), and that makes these words so bittersweet:

> Longin' to tell you, but afraid and shy,
> I let my golden chances pass me by.
> Now I've lost you, soon I will go in the mist of day,
> And you *never* will know *how* I loved you,
> *How* I loved you!

Billy had let all his *todays* slip by until it was too late to let Julie know just how much he loved her.

This story might seem like romantic mush to many people, but I find in it a moving reminder of the importance of today. Maybe the importance of today means holding someone close to us and saying, "I love you." Maybe it means placing that phone call we have intended to make. Maybe it means obeying a truth of Scripture that has been ringing in our hearts. Possibly it means stepping out to obey the prompting of God's Spirit.

Whatever the case might be, you and I have only one day to do what God is calling us to do, and that day is today. Let's not allow one more day of opportunity to pass us by.

As long as it is called today, let us serve the Lord and love others with all of our hearts.

❦

Heavenly Father, we thank you for the blessings and opportunities of today. Help us to live each day of our lives with the wisdom that only you can give. Don't let us miss doing your will today because of worry about tomorrow or regrets about the past. Give us grace to trust you day by day, for we ask this all in Jesus' name, amen.

FIVE

❧

Making It Through
the Storm

WALWYN STUART, THE PORT AUTHORITY POLICE OFFI-
CER, was not the only Brooklyn Tabernacle church member we lost in the attacks on the World Trade Center.

Boyie Mohammed was a fairly new convert to Christ
who worked as a trader with Carr Futures on the ninety-
fourth floor of the North Tower. Originally from Trinidad,
West Indies, he and his wife, Lynette, had been attending
our church for several years, along with their two grown
children.

A twenty-three-year veteran with the New York City
Fire Department, Ronnie Henderson was a firefighter with
Engine 279, Ladder Company No. 131. His firehouse on
Lorraine Street in Red Hook, Brooklyn, was one of the first
to respond to the attacks and the ensuing fires. He lived
north of the city, more than ninety miles from our church,
but that didn't stop Ronnie from worshiping with us every
Sunday and learning more about Jesus. He was very serious
about his faith in God, and it affected every aspect of his life.
Fifty-two-year-old Ronnie left behind his wife, Shirley, two
grown sons, a grown daughter, and a fifteen-year-old son.

When we talk about *everyone's* life being changed by the horrific scene of death and destruction at Ground Zero, Ebony Wright belongs near the top of that list. A nineteen-year-old who attends our church, Ebony is a sophomore in college majoring in sociology. When she was not attending school in Hartford, Connecticut, she would go to her home on Adelphi Street in downtown Brooklyn and be with her mother, Sandra.

Sandra had raised Ebony, her only child, all by herself. She was not only Ebony's mother, but also her best friend. Sandra had been a member of our church for several years and worked at the World Trade Center. On September 11 she went to the offices of Cantor Fitzgerald, the well-known bond firm located on floors 101–105 in the North Tower. When American Airlines Flight 11 blasted into those floors at 8:47 that morning, none of the 730 employees in the workstations and offices of Cantor Fitzgerald survived. In a split second, Ebony lost her mother, her best friend, and the one person who had financially supported every part of her life.

What now?

The Brooklyn Tabernacle—including the pastoral staff and several couples in leadership—continues to minister to each family in the church directly affected by the terrorist attacks. This help and ministry takes many forms. Carol and I, along with the entire congregation, have "adopted" Ebony. She will eat at our home this Thanksgiving Day. Whatever she needs, in days and months and years to come, the congregation will be there for her. We can care for her, but we can't replace her mother, and we know it.

Even people not directly affected by the attacks, however, are having a hard time of it. America is definitely at war, and the horrible carnage and unknown nature of the terrorist conflict have cast a pall of sorrow, gloom, and deep anxiety across the United States. If that weren't enough, add the resulting uncertainties of the stock market and the ripple effects of the terrorist attacks on the entire economy. People are now asking themselves questions they never would have considered before September 11: *Is it safe to take my vacation and fly on a commercial airline? Where and when will the next terrorist attack occur? If my company cuts back, will I lose my job? Dare I open my mail and risk contracting anthrax? What kind of world will my children (or grandchildren) grow up in?* The people of this nation are going through a very dark storm.

DO NOT LOSE HEART

With questions such as these swirling about and new pressures bearing down on us, it is important that we ponder God's directive for making it through this storm. Although he lived in another time and place, the apostle Paul faced intense seasons of life filled with trials of various kinds. He was repeatedly persecuted, beaten, and jailed. He experienced strong opposition almost everywhere he preached the gospel of Jesus Christ. He suffered physical privation and continually risked his life. He also had to deal with the mental and emotional anguish that resulted from troubles within the new churches he had founded. But Paul not only made it through the storm, he did so victoriously and with unwavering obedience to the Lord's call on his life.

When any of us pass through a difficult season of life, there is a strong tendency to *lose heart*. Paul recognized this problem as he reviewed his own battles and outlined a remedy. "Therefore, since through God's mercy we have this ministry, we do not *lose heart*. . . . But we have this treasure [the life of Christ through the Holy Spirit's presence] in *jars of clay* to show that this all-surpassing power is *from God* and *not from us*. We are *hard pressed* on every side, but not crushed; *perplexed*, but not in despair" (2 Corinthians 4:1, 7–8).

> **The crucial thing, according to the apostle Paul, is not to lose heart.**
>
> ❧

The crucial thing, according to Paul, is not to lose heart. The conflicts and adversities we face are very real, but with God's help we can avoid the fatal step of giving up. The Greek word Paul used here means to become "spiritless, discouraged, exhausted, and wearied out through fear." Losing heart is a clear and present danger for everyone today, but we Christians especially must not succumb. We can't afford to "become weary in doing good" (Galatians 6:9) because today is a unique moment of spiritual harvest. We must dig down deeply into God and find new strength in him so we will "never tire of doing what is right" (2 Thessalonians 3:13). We can't afford to lose our Christian witness or miss out on ministry opportunities because of spiritual fatigue.

Of course we are susceptible to losing heart, or Paul would never have accented this thought twice in this one chapter (2 Corinthians 4:1, 16). The reality is, no one is a superman or superwoman despite the fact that they might be born-again believers. In fact, our life as Christians uniquely merges two seemingly contradictory truths.

First, Christ lives *in us* through the presence of the Holy Spirit, and as God directs us into his will we *can* do all things through Christ. Second, Scripture also states that "we have this treasure in jars of clay," which highlights our human vulnerability to pain and hardship.

No one today is more spiritual than the apostle was or possesses greater faith than he had. Yet he candidly related how his "jar of clay" was hedged in and oppressed in every way imaginable. But hard-pressed as he was, Paul was never so cramped in or crushed that he couldn't serve God triumphantly. Yes, he faced many perplexities that even drove him to the point of being "unable to find a way out" (2 Corinthians 4:8 AMPLIFIED BIBLE). But by God's grace, Paul was never driven to such despair that he caved in and quit!

By the way, all that teaching about a "faith formula" that will spare us from any trouble or emotional pain seems rather ridiculous nowadays, doesn't it? The reality is that the current crisis highlights our vulnerability and humanness, even for us believers. We can be devoted Christians and still die suddenly in the middle of life, as Stephen did (Acts 7:59–60). We can love God and still cry real tears. We can have faith in the Lord and still battle with anxiety about our families and our future. Christians have real emotions and go through storms like everyone else. And it's not a bad thing to admit it, either.

A TIME TO REFLECT LIGHT IN THE DARKNESS

I bear witness to Paul's words about the fragile nature of our human condition. As a New Yorker and an American, I have been deeply affected by the recent tragedies. I found myself crying the other day when I saw a mother crossing the street with her little boy on the way to school. I could not help but think about the hundreds of children who will be raised without dads or moms and the hundreds of women and men who are now widowed. I have crossed the Manhattan Bridge and seen the altered skyline with that acrid smoke still slowly ascending into the air above Ground Zero. Who would not weep at these scenes? Who would not be deeply affected by the thought of such a demonic hatred existing in our world?

> **Our fragile, vulnerable lives are the showcase of God's supernatural grace.**
>
> ∞

But it is of no value to curse the darkness. As Christians we need to light the candle of eternal hope that is at the heart of the gospel. Ebony and others like her are walking through one of the severest storms life can offer. But even so, she is not going to lose heart and quit, because Christ is going to uphold her. That is how God designed it to be. Our fragile, vulnerable lives are the showcase of his supernatural grace so others will know that "this all-surpassing power *is from God* and *not from us*" (2 Corinthians 4:7).

Ebony's future, and the futures of so many Christians impacted by tragedy, will testify that God's promises are real and can be relied upon. And the Lord, in turn, will be exalted because it will be evident that it's a *supernatural* power, not a *natural* power, that enables her, and others like her, to walk bravely through the storm.

WE NEED INNER RENEWAL DAILY

But what is the exact process that keeps God's people from "going under" in the face of the intense strain of perilous circumstances? The answer to this question involves another truth that God is reminding people everywhere to carefully think about: "Therefore we do not lose heart, but though our *outer man* is decaying, yet our *inner man* is being renewed *day by day*" (2 Corinthians 4:16 NASB).

Paul definitely knew his "outer man" was part of his existence here on earth. The outer man is the vulnerable, physical part of us. No matter how many vitamin supplements we take or what kind of shape we are in, by its very nature the outer man is progressively wasting away. The day of our death is inevitable—and we are closer to it than we were yesterday.

Paul's outer man was beaten, put in chains, and grew weary. It was susceptible to pain and discomfort, which in turn attacked his willingness to continue on the path of obedience to God. But there was more to Paul than his outer man, just as there is more to each of us. Almighty God created human beings as more than mere physical bodies. Within Paul, just as there is within us, there was an "inner man" of the heart. Paul testified that despite what was happening to the outer man, the inner man was being "renewed day by day." On a daily basis the grace of God was imparted to his inner spirit, which enabled him to be "strong *in the Lord* and in his mighty power" (Ephesians 6:10). In the same way, God's supernatural presence can work within our hearts today. God's grace can renew our hearts and enable us to stand strong against the violent winds blowing through the land.

Unfortunately, the reality and importance of our spiritual side is often overlooked. It is sad to think about, but we devote an inordinate amount of time to our outer man while often neglecting the condition of our inner man. How we look, the clothes we wear, the weight we try to maintain, our cholesterol levels, and so much more consume our daily thoughts. But what good is perfect physical health if inside we are spiritually weak and undernourished? What's the benefit of being in good shape if spiritually we are devoid of faith and are gradually losing heart?

If we are going to live effectively as salt and light, we need an overhaul of our spiritual lives. We must have new, strong doses of the Word of God. We need a revival of personal prayer and waiting before the Lord. We need more edifying fellowship with other believers, along with heartfelt worship and praise to God. But we require all these things on a *daily basis* because the renewal of the inner man occurs "day by day." Let us pray that God will begin a fresh work inside all of us so we can join with the psalmist in proclaiming, "God is the *strength of my heart*" (Psalm 73:26).

TEMPORARY TROUBLES, ETERNAL GLORY

The contrast between the outer man and the inner man is not the only contrast Paul highlighted in this passage. He went on to explain that there's a huge difference between *temporary troubles* and *eternal glory*: "For our light and momentary troubles are achieving for us an eternal glory that far outweighs them all" (2 Corinthians 4:17). It almost takes my breath away to remember that Paul was repeatedly beaten and jailed, and once left for dead, yet he referred to these trials as "light and momentary troubles"! The only reason Paul could describe his troubles this way is that through the eyes of faith he saw something greater. He had caught a glimpse of the incredible, eternal reward waiting for every Christian. The transcendent glory of heaven was "beyond all measure" and "excessively surpassing all comparisons and all calculations" (2 Corinthians 4:17 AMPLIFIED BIBLE).

The daily renewal of Paul's inner man opened up his eyes of faith and made eternity real to him. Heaven, in fact, became more real than the physical world and trials that surrounded him. This was no weird "pie-in-the-sky" religion. The eyes of Paul's heart simply perceived glorious, spiritual realities that can never be revealed to the physical senses. So when he compared what he knew of eternal glory to all the difficulties he was going through, Paul could calmly call them "light and momentary troubles."

Many pastors and Christians have shied away from teaching this truth because it sounds a bit mystical. But the current wave of terrorism is a powerful reminder that this truth is not optional. Instead, it is mandatory to "fix our eyes not on what is seen, but on what is unseen. For what is seen is temporary, but what is unseen is eternal" (2 Corinthians 4:18). If you and I only focus on what is *visible*, how can we possibly avoid anxiety and fear? Skyscrapers are coming down. Financial markets are unsure. Unknown enemies might strike again at any moment. Life on earth is a vapor at best. How can we have peace and joy if our hearts cling to this earth and the things in it?

> **What we view as our ultimate reality will determine how well we make it through the storm.**
>
> ❧

The new terrorist war is forcing people throughout the world to think about time and eternity. God wants us—every one of us—to compare the security of temporary, material things with the glorious, eternal reward awaiting believers in heaven. What we view as our ultimate reality will determine how well we make it through the storm. We can choose to live for the here and now, or we can choose to fix our spiritual eyes and hearts on where Christ is, seated at the right hand of God (Romans 8:34; Hebrews 1:3).

The chaos that is now present in the world, and the possibility of future terror, can sometimes be overwhelming. It seems as if our world has somehow slipped out of orbit, and the future appears dark. Ominous clouds loom overheard. But as believers in Christ, we must remember that he often walks toward us on the same stormy seas that threaten to capsize our boat. Many unanswered questions tempt us to fear, but other questions give us reason to hope.

Those questions—and their answers—are found in God's Word and were written for our encouragement:

> Do you not know?
>> Have you not heard?
> Has it not been told you from the beginning?
>> Have you not understood since the earth was founded?
> *He sits enthroned* above the circle of the earth,
>> and its people are like grasshoppers. . . .
> He brings princes to naught
>> and reduces the rulers of this world to nothing. . . .
> "To whom will you compare *me*?
>> Or who is my equal?" says the Holy One. . . .
> Why do you say, O Jacob,
>> and complain, O Israel,
> "My way is hidden from the LORD;
>> my cause is disregarded by my God"?
> Do you not know?
>> Have you not heard?
> The LORD is the *everlasting* God,
>> the Creator of the ends of the earth. . . .
> He gives *strength to the weary*
>> and *increases the power of the weak*. . . .
> *Those who hope* in *the LORD*
>> *will renew their strength*.
> *They will soar* on wings like eagles;
>> *they will run* and not grow weary,
>> *they will walk* and not be faint." —ISAIAH 40:21–23, 25, 27–29, 31

By God's grace we will walk victoriously through the storm!

SIX

∽

A Strange Blessing

SEVERAL OF THE NEW YORK CITY NEWSPAPERS have been running daily series on some of the people who perished as a result of the World Trade Center attacks. One edition will feature photographs and biographical sketches of the valiant police officers and firefighters who gave their lives attempting to rescue others. Another edition will feature photographs of some of the thousands of employees who never made it out of the Twin Towers.

But the stories of the almost five thousand people who died there or at the Pentagon are not the only stories worth noting. There are numerous accounts of people who managed to escape the disaster scene even though they worked on the seventy-fifth or ninety-second floor. Like Dawn Robinson, they exited the North or South Tower just minutes, or even seconds, before the fire, smoke, or collapse of the building would have snuffed out their lives. It seems as if everyone knows someone who "got out just in time."

There are also other, unusual stories circulating through the offices, churches, and neighborhoods of our city. These are the stories of people who, because of unusual circumstances, were not at their normal workplaces on September 11, 2001. A representative of a firm head-quartered in the World Trade Center, for example, was on a business trip he really didn't want to make. On that Tuesday he was on an airplane bound for Toronto at the same time that his office and the entire floor on which he worked was obliterated in a few seconds. A stalled car kept a woman from being in her usual place of employment at 2 World Trade Center. A terrible flu bug kept another person from going to work on that fateful day.

> **Seemingly negative or frustrating experiences often yield beneficial results we never could have imagined.**
>
> ❧

These stories remind us of a strange but true fact. Seemingly negative or frustrating experiences often yield beneficial results we never could have imagined.

We should not be terribly surprised by this because the Word of God unequivocally asserts, "A man's steps are directed by the LORD. How then can anyone understand his own way?" (Proverbs 20:24). This statement is obviously both true *and* mysterious. What we plan to do is not always what ends up happening. God is *sovereign* and. when he is not allowed to rule, he overrules circumstances to accomplish his purposes on the earth.

Also, the Lord often leads us into situations that appear to be very different from what we would have imagined or desired. Again, this should not surprise us, because he has already explained why this will occur: "'For my thoughts are not your thoughts, *neither are your ways my ways*,' declares the LORD. 'As the heavens are higher than the earth, so are *my ways higher than your ways* and my thoughts than your thoughts'" (Isaiah 55:8–9). G. Campbell Morgan, a noted British expositor, once said, in effect, "When all my exegesis fails, I worship." For us that means this: We do not always understand *what* is going on, but we can still rest in the assurance that we know *who* sits on the throne and reigns supreme.

Almighty God permits many unexplainable things in a world in which he has created people who exercise free will. We cannot put all the pieces of the puzzle together yet, because, as the apostle Paul wrote, "Now we see but a poor reflection as in a mirror; *then* we shall see face to face. Now I know *in part; then* I shall know fully, even as I am fully known" (1 Corinthians 13:12). There will be a moment in the future—the *"then"* to which Paul refers—when we will comprehend all the apparent mysteries of life on earth. Until *then*, however, we must walk by faith. We must keep trusting in God, whose ways are often inscrutable yet always governed by his divine love.

This is why the apostle Paul, after expounding on the most profound mysteries involving God and man, suddenly broke out into worshipful praise:

> Oh, the depth of the riches of the wisdom and knowledge of God!
> How *unsearchable* his judgments,
> and his paths *beyond tracing out!*

"Who has known the mind of the Lord?
    Or who has been his counselor?"
"Who has ever given to God,
    that God should repay him?"
For from him and through him and to him are all things.
    To him be the glory forever! Amen. —ROMANS 11:33–36

As my friend Warren Wiersbe once told me, "When you have problems with theology, try doxology!" Sometimes we just have to bow our hearts and worship God.

PERSPECTIVE

It is not only tragic world events such as those we witnessed on September 11 that cause us to pause and ponder the "whys" behind things. Sometimes God's dealings with his own people can also be very difficult to figure out. For example, Jesus said that there were many widows in Israel during the severe famine associated with the prophet Elijah, "yet Elijah was not sent to any of them, but to a widow in Zarephath in the region of Sidon" (Luke 4:26; see 1 Kings 17:7–24). Why did God not send relief and blessing to a widow among the chosen people of Israel? Why did he choose an obscure Gentile woman in Sidon to be the beneficiary of his grace? No reason is given in Scripture, nor will we comprehend it this side of heaven.

Consider also why, if Jesus loved Lazarus so dearly, it is written, "Yet when he [Jesus] heard that Lazarus was sick, he stayed where he was two more days" (John 11:6). Jesus' inaction certainly baffled the disciples, but there *was* a reason for Jesus to respond exactly as he did that they soon understood. Mary and Martha, the sisters of Lazarus, at first were hurt by Jesus' seeming lack of concern, but they eventually realized that it all worked out "for God's glory" (v. 4). People standing near

> **Sometimes God's dealings with his own people can be very difficult to figure out.**
> ❧

Lazarus' tomb saw the glory of God (v. 40) and had the opportunity to believe that Jesus is the Son of God (v. 42). There is an old saying that helps us keep the right perspective: "Our *disappointments* are often God's *appointments*."

DIVINE TRAINING

I recently read an obscure passage of Scripture that opened up, in a new way, my understanding of how God works.

Joshua, who succeeded Moses as the leader of Israel, had led the people across the Jordan River in order to possess the Promised Land. The book of Joshua records the key battles the Israelites fought as they drove out the idolatrous Canaanite tribes. At the end of his life, Joshua made a farewell speech in which he looked back over Israel's history and reminded the people of God's sovereign and gracious dealing with "father Abraham" and his descendants. God used Joshua prophetically as he spoke to the Israelites: "This is what the LORD, the God of Israel, says: '. . . I took your father Abraham from the land beyond the River and led him throughout Canaan and gave him many descendants'" (Joshua 24:2–3). There's a lot of history packed into that one sentence!

Although Abraham came from a family of idolaters, God sovereignly chose him to be the earthly father of his chosen people. God blessed Abraham in his old age by giving a son, Isaac (Genesis 21:1–7), who later had twin sons, Jacob and Esau (Genesis 25:21–26). God so cherished Abraham and his descendants that one of God's descriptive names for himself is "the God of Abraham, Isaac, and Jacob" (see Exodus 3:6, 15; 4:5). Notice that there is no mention of Esau in that name. Indeed, it is in the account of Jehovah choosing Jacob instead of Esau that we confront one of God's mysterious, unusual ways of blessing his children.

"To Isaac I gave Jacob and Esau," God said. "I assigned *the hill country of Seir to Esau*, but *Jacob and his sons* went down *to Egypt*" (Joshua 24:4). God had chosen Jacob *over* Esau to inherit the divine blessing given to Abraham. Jacob's descendants, not Esau's, would possess the Promised Land. So why did the Lord assign "the hill country of Seir" to Esau? Seir—also known as Edom—was the hill country southeast of the Promised Land. Although it was not a fertile area for farming, it was mountainous and easy to defend against enemies. How can we explain why, if Jehovah *rejected Esau* as the heir of his special blessing, God gave the land of Seir to Esau while Jacob and his sons were shipped off to *Egypt?* If Jacob was so special to God (as in "the God of Abraham, Isaac, and *Jacob*")—if God would later change Jacob's name to "Israel" (Genesis 32:22–28), why did God send him to Egypt? Why didn't God just give the Promised Land to Jacob at the beginning?

The trip to Egypt began well enough because God, using what first appeared to be awful circumstances (Genesis 37; 39–42), sent Joseph before them and promoted him to Pharaoh's right hand. But as the years rolled by, *Joseph* became a forgotten name, and the Hebrews became too numerous for their own good. The Egyptians enslaved them, and Pharaoh became vehement in his fear and hatred of the Hebrews. So, for the Hebrews, Egypt eventually became a place of slavery, suffering, and the edict decreeing death to all newborn sons (Exodus 1:22).

Now here is what is difficult for us. We know God has *all power* and also *knows all things.* So how did Jacob's descendants make sense of the Lord's "special favor" toward them as they toiled to make bricks under the hot, Egyptian sun? Why did God permit, even orchestrate, their stay for hundreds of years in Egypt if they were his "chosen ones"? Doesn't it seem that Esau, the "rejected" son, actually got the better end of the deal? I'm afraid that many of our modern-day "prophets" would have explained the seeming inequity as being the result of the Hebrews' "national sin" even though they weren't yet a nation!

Let's not forget that God's ways of dealing with people on earth are far too complex to fit into our simplistic religious formulas. Contrary to what some Christians teach, a tragedy like this cannot be declared unequivocally as judgment on this nation or chastisement for an individual because of some sin or misbehavior. Yes, the Bible records many examples of sinful sowing followed by a sure and horrible reaping, but not everything in life can be so easily categorized. As was the case with Job in the Old Testament, many tragedies have no discernible, spiritual cause, and we do well to remember this truth. Who can say with certainty why Walwyn Stuart and three other members of our church died that day while Dawn Robinson and others escaped at the last moment? We will have to content ourselves with the knowledge that our sovereign God is at work and recognize the future hope emphasized in the lyrics of the old gospel song: "We will understand it better by and by."

> **Although God's ways may baffle us in the present, the lens of history often enables us to see some benefit in these same circumstances.**
>
> ❧

Although God's ways may baffle us in the present, the lens of history often enables us to see some benefit in these same circumstances. Let's consider, for example, a few things that happened while the Israelites sojourned in Egypt as part of God's plan for them. The Bible says that "the *more they were oppressed*, the *more they multiplied and spread*; so the Egyptians came to dread the Israelites" (Exodus 1:12). Through the ongoing hardships of life in Egypt, the enslaved Israelites developed a resiliency and endurance that became part of their national character. The more difficult their life situation became, the more they clung to the promises of blessing God had given to their forefathers. Instead of hopelessly caving in, they persevered through God's power. The "Egypt experience" put iron in their soul.

This truth has helped me to better understand a thousand and one difficulties the Lord has permitted Carol and me to go through. She and I began our ministry with a handful of people in a rundown church building in the inner city. We received a salary of only $3,800 the first year, and we were confronted with many problems. It was an overwhelming experience that challenged our willingness to fulfill God's calling on our lives. Several times during those early years I wanted to quit, but God helped me to hold on to his promises and not run. When I look back *now*, I see that those difficult years were a time of invaluable, divine training. A tenacious faith was birthed in us. We learned, among other things, that God *would come through* no matter how bleak things looked around us.

Perseverance is never produced through easy, sunny days that present no challenges. You and I learn to endure by tightly holding on to God through trials and severe challenges. That is how God shaped every outstanding man and woman in the Bible, and we see the same pattern repeated throughout every century of church history. If Jesus, the Son of God, "learned obedience from what *he suffered*" (Hebrews 5:8), then how can there be a *different process* for those of us who are called by his name? All the men and women whom God blesses and prepares for meaningful ministry *must* go down to their own "Egypt" for a season.

NOWHERE TO TURN BUT TO GOD

Another divine purpose connected to the stay of God's people in Egypt has to do with *prayer*. Although we read that Abraham, Isaac, and Jacob all built altars and worshiped Jehovah at times, something new happened in

Egypt. The Hebrews were so abused and misused that they had nowhere to turn but to God. In their utter powerlessness, they began to pray with desperation and fervency.

When God appeared to Moses in the burning bush, he commissioned the Hebrew shepherd to return to Egypt and deliver his people from bondage. What preceded this encounter, however, was the real origin of God's intervention on behalf of the Hebrew people. "During that long period, the king of Egypt died. The Israelites groaned in their slavery and *cried out*, and *their cry for help* because of their slavery *went up to God*. God heard their groaning" (Exodus 2:23–24).

When the Hebrews called out desperately for divine deliverance, Jehovah took notice because of his nature as a prayer-answering God. He then told Moses: "And now the *cry of the Israelites has reached me.* . . . So now, go. I am sending you to Pharaoh to bring my people the Israelites out of Egypt" (Exodus 3:9–10). This collective cry for help became part of Israel's character and was repeated often throughout its history.

When Moses was ready to pass out of this life many years later, he reminded Israel of what stood out most about them as a nation: "What other nation is so great as to have their gods near them the way the LORD our God *is near us* whenever *we pray to him?*" (Deuteronomy 4:7). We need to remember that the Israelites' deep consciousness of the power of prayer began not in the "land of milk and honey," but during their years of hardship in Egypt. Their instinctive response of turning to prayer as the key ingredient of spiritual survival was planted in their hearts by God himself. He laid this down in Scripture as a first principle: "*Call upon me* in the day of trouble; I will deliver you, and you will honor me" (Psalm 50:15).

> *Anything*—and I mean *anything*—becomes a blessing if it drives us to prayer.
> ∝

This principle is the key to many of God's mysterious dealings with us. *Anything*—and I mean *anything*—becomes a blessing if it drives us to prayer. God has not changed one iota in thousands of years: "The same Lord is Lord of all and *richly blesses all who call on him*" (Romans 10:12). God wants to pour his grace out on you and me, on our nation, and on the whole world. But his blessing is contingent on whether or not we open our hearts and humbly reach out to the Almighty in *prayer*.

When pressed against the wall and facing possible death, it's amazing how many men and women call out to God. That is why we have this old adage: "There are no atheists in a foxhole."

Have you noticed what has been happening all across the land since September 11? God is using the unpredictable threat of terrorism to make the whole country a foxhole! People are praying everywhere. They are not even ashamed to pray in public. Many people who before September 11 doubted God's existence are now groping to find him. Bible sales are off the charts. Those who have never before attended church are now filling the pews. Couldn't this be another illustration of the principle so often mentioned in

Scripture: "*He will call upon me*, and I will answer him; I will be with him *in trouble*" (Psalm 91:15)?

A PERSONAL WAKE-UP CALL

Has the Lord gotten your attention yet? Are you still putting off getting right with God until tomorrow? Are you continuing to live far away from Christ even though it means forfeiting his plan for your life?

Today the Lord is calling us back to himself. He is prompting us to refocus on eternity and heaven instead of being preoccupied with temporary, material things. God has given us a new *today*, and we must use it to draw near to him.

Darker days filled with more turmoil and anxiety may be ahead. Many people might lose heart because of fear. Who knows what tomorrow may bring forth—physically, politically, or economically? Now that towering, seemingly impregnable skyscrapers have come crashing to the ground, who can confidently predict the future?

God longs for us to place our faith in him, to trust him no matter what happens around us. And we can know, with absolute certainty, that he is at work. Yes, his ways are not our ways, but they are the *best* ways.

God is in the business of redeeming men and women, boys and girls. One day there will be no more tears and pain. One day those of us who have placed our trust in Jesus as Savior and Lord will see the glory of God revealed, and we will fully experience his love. Until then, we have today—the first day in the rest of our lives—and how we use it will make all the difference.

Our God is still able to carry us through the storm with a song on our lips. As the prophet Habakkuk wrote eloquently so many years ago:

> Though the fig tree does not bud
> and there are no grapes on the vines,
> though the olive crop fails
> and the fields produce no food,
> though there are no sheep in the pen
> and no cattle in the stalls,
> *yet I will rejoice in the LORD,*
> I will be joyful in God my Savior. —HABAKKUK 3:17

❧

Heavenly Father, we appreciate and worship you as we go through difficult times that are hard to understand. We surrender ourselves into your hand and pray that your name might be exalted through our lives. Finally, help us to have faith during the hard times and to give thanks in everything. In Jesus' name, amen.

FRESH FAITH

*What Happens When Real Faith
Ignites God's People*

JIM CYMBALA
WITH DEAN MERRILL

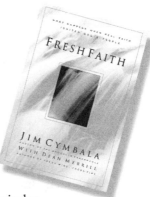

In an era laced with worry about the present and cynicism about the future, in a climate in which we've grown tired of hoping for miracles and wary of trumped-up claims that only disappoint, comes a confident reminder that God has not fallen asleep. He has not forgotten his people nor retreated into semi-retirement. On the contrary, he is ready to respond to real faith wherever he finds it.

Pastor Jim Cymbala insists that authentic, biblical faith is simple, honest, and utterly dependent upon God, a faith capable of transforming your life, your church, and the nation itself.

Jim Cymbala calls us back to the authentic, biblical faith—a fiery, passionate preoccupation with God that will restore our troubled children, our wounded marriages, and our broken and divided churches. Born out of the heart and soul of the Brooklyn Tabernacle, the message of *Fresh Faith* is illustrated by true stories of men and women whose lives have been changed through the power of faith.

Hardcover 0-310-23007-1
Audio Pages® Abridged Cassettes 0-310-23006-3
Audio Pages® Unabridged CD 0-310-23639-8

Pick up a copy today at your favorite bookstore!

FRESH POWER

*Experiencing the Vast Resources
of the Spirit of God*

JIM CYMBALA
WITH DEAN MERRILL

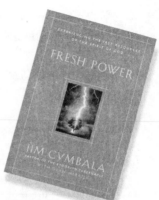

Pastor Jim Cymbala of the Brooklyn
Tabernacle has taught his congregation how God's mighty power can
infuse their present-day lives and the
mission of their church. He contin-
ued that teaching nationally in his best-selling
books *Fresh Wind, Fresh Fire* and *Fresh Faith*, which tell
about the transforming power of God's love to convert prostitutes,
addicts, the homeless, and people of all races and stations in life.

Now in *Fresh Power* Cymbala continues to spread the word
about the power of God's Holy Spirit in the lives of those who
seek him. Fresh power, Cymbala says, is available to us as we
desire the Holy Spirit's constant infilling and learn what it means
to be Spirit filled, both as individuals and as the church. With the
book of Acts as the basis for his study, Cymbala shows how the
daily lives of first-century Christians were defined by their belief
in God's Word, in the constant infilling of his Spirit, and in the
clear and direct responses of obedience to Scripture. He shows
that that same life in Christ through the power of the Holy Spirit
is available today for pastors, leaders, and lay people who are
longing for revival.

Hardcover 0-310-23008-X
Audio Pages® Abridged Cassettes 0-310-23467-X
Audio Pages® Unabridged CD 0-310-24200-2

THE LIFE GOD BLESSES

*The Secret of Enjoying
God's Favor*

JIM CYMBALA
WITH STEPHEN SORENSON

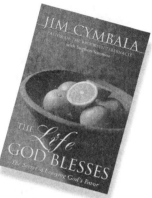

God Wants to Bless Your Life!

Think of what it means to have God
bless your family, your relationships,
your ministry, your finances ...
every aspect of your life. Think how
wonderful it would be to have the Creator of the
universe "show himself strong" on your behalf.

Good news! That's exactly what he wants to do. God is so
eager to bless people that he's constantly searching for that special kind of heart on which he can pour out his goodness. Yours
can be that kind of heart.

Pastor Jim Cymbala shares stories from the Bible and from
the lives of men and women he has known to reveal inner qualities that delight your heavenly Father. Cultivate them in your
heart and stand amazed as God answers your most heartfelt
prayers and makes the impossible come true in your life.

Hardcover 0-310-24202-9

Pick up a copy today at your favorite bookstore!

ZONDERVAN™

GRAND RAPIDS, MICHIGAN 49530

w w w . z o n d e r v a n . c o m

THE CHURCH GOD BLESSES

Available March 2002

JIM CYMBALA
WITH STEPHEN SORENSON

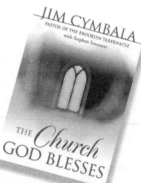

God wants to transform his church into a people of power, joy, and peace.

Jim Cymbala reminds us that Christianity is only as strong as the local church and that God wants to bless our churches in ways we can't possibly imagine. It doesn't matter whether a church is alive and growing or barely surviving on life support. God has a plan for it.

As the pastor of the Brooklyn Tabernacle, Cymbala knows that God's blessing and grace is available to us today just as much as it was in the early church, when thousands of people became believers despite the fact that the church lacked everything we consider vital: church buildings, seminaries, printed materials, sound systems, choirs, and money. None of these things mattered. What mattered was that God's hand was on the church, working through his people to build the kingdom.

In this second book of a three-book series on the way God wants to pour out his blessings, best-selling author Jim Cymbala describes the kind of church God wants to bless and use mightily for his kingdom. Cymbala, who has seen his church grow from a handful of the faithful to a vibrant, multi-ethnic and growing beacon of hope in the city, believes that God desires to bless the church but that the church is often more interested in programs and "fads."

Cymbala outlines the qualities that God is looking for in the church and shows how any church can become a vessel for God's blessings. Through the use of stories from his own congregation and this pastor's wise insights from Scripture, this book will satisfy the hunger every Christian has to see the church become what God intended it to be.

Hardcover 0-310-24203-7

HE'S BEEN FAITHFUL

Trusting God to Do What
Only He Can Do

CAROL CYMBALA
WITH ANN SPANGLER

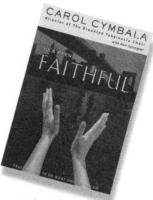

Carol Cymbala's ministry in a tough inner-city neighborhood in New York can be summed up in one word: unlikely. She is the director and songwriter for a Grammy Award-winning choir—yet she doesn't read music. She is the pastor's wife in a 6,000-member congregation filled with people of color—and she is white. A shy girl who struggled to get through school, she is the last person you'd expect to stand before a packed house at Radio City Music Hall, confidently directing the Brooklyn Tabernacle Choir.

But Carol's God is the God of the unlikely. *He's Been Faithful* is an honest story about the struggles we all face and the power of God to help us. It is told through Carol's eyes as well as through the eyes of various members of the Brooklyn Tabernacle Choir who have experienced the grace of Christ in remarkable ways. *He's Been Faithful* tells the story of the way God works despite—or maybe because of—our many inadequacies.

But Carol's faith hasn't always come easily. There have been times of wavering and challenge, like the time a man walked down the aisle of the church pointing a gun at her husband, Jim. Or like the time she was assaulted outside the church. Or like the time she wanted to pack up her children and run away from the city for good because of what was happening to her family.

Whether you are a pastor, a choir director, or someone who is seeking a deeper experience of God, *He's Been Faithful* will renew your faith and increase your understanding that only Jesus can fill that deep, deep longing we all have for something more in life.

Hardcover 0-310-23652-5
Audio Pages® Abridged Cassettes 0-310-23668-1

We want to hear from you. Please send your comments about this
book to us in care of the address below. Thank you.

ZONDERVAN™

GRAND RAPIDS, MICHIGAN 49530

www.zondervan.com